# BRILLIANT GARDENS

# BRILLIANT GARDENS

## A CELEBRATION OF ENGLISH GARDENING

CANDIDA LYCETT GREEN

AND

ANDREW LAWSON

Chatto & Windus

LONDON

Printed in 1989 by
Chatto & Windus
30 Bedford Square
London WC1B 3SG

A CIP record for this book is available from the
British Library.

ISBN 0 7011 3268 X

Colour origination by Scantrans, Singapore
Photoset by Rowland Phototypesetting,
Bury St Edmunds, Suffolk

Printed by Roundwood Press, Warwick

HALF TITLE
Mr and Mrs Abel's garden, Netherhampton Road, Salisbury

TITLE PAGE
Mr J. Beveridge's concrete menagerie, Brankstone,
Cornhill-on-Tweed, Northumberland

# INTRODUCTION

Our small gardens are the best in the world. It's not just that we have the greenest fingers or that our climate produces beautiful roses, hollyhocks and apple trees but because we are born with a love of gardening in our veins. It is as deep rooted as our oaks and, though it does not always burgeon, it is there waiting just beneath the soil.

The French pack their plots with enviable endives, celeriac and mange-touts; they prune their fruit trees to espaliered perfection against wall and picket fence. The Italians graze their goats beneath olive trees, display the most rampant geraniums and grow the most voluptuous vines beneath which to dine. But we English want to show the world how *artistic* we are. We have not quite mastered the art of cooking, nor of graceful relaxation but, as gardeners, we want to show off our industriousness, our horticultural expertise and, most of all, our art.

This book is not about the great gardens of houses and palaces like Hestercombe and Hampton Court. Those established wonders will be maintained for our childrens' children to enjoy; their beauty, scale and grandeur are such that they will always be nurtured by troupes of gardeners and their glories written of, painted and photographed for posterity. This book is about the myriad small and often transient masterpieces which go unrecorded. It is about the gardens upon which our just reputation as a nation of great gardeners is based. If you travel through wild Northumbrian moorland villages, through quiet Lincolnshire fenland or round London's North Circular Road skirting Wembley and Chingford, you will see, every so often, a garden which makes you stop in your tracks or fall off your bicycle or crash into the car in front. It is these exceptional gardens which I like to boast about. They may be tumblingly romantic, gaudily formal, intricately ornamental but, whatever their style, they are what I would define as pretty blooming brilliant!

If your cottage is of mellow brick and thatch or weathered Cotswold stone, then the atmosphere of your garden is half set. But it is hard to start from scratch in front of a brand new house on an estate. So much has been done over the last twenty years to erode the local character of England. The virtual standardisation of cheap building materials means that the same bricks, window frames, tiles and front doors are used in Birmingham and Bristol, in Newcastle and Torquay. Our High Streets lose their regional identity daily as a dreary same-

1

ness pervades, with identical signage and shops obsessed with corporate imagery. But somehow, despite the spread of garden centre chains which all sell exactly the same African violets, bird seed, bright green plastic plant ties and employ people who seldom know about plants but prefer the 'sundry' side of things, our gardeners still fly their own aspidistras. They save their own seed, bring on their own bedding plants, make their own cement figures and shape their own hedges. Knowledge is passed on from father to son, from neighbour to neighbour. No two gardens are ever the same, however alike the houses.

Very formal gardens are the most popular. This is not at all surprising: but for the odd lurch into informality, Europe has always been in love with symmetry. In the 1480s the great architectural theorist Leon Battista Alberti suggested that every villa should have a garden laid out in geometrical patterns and that it should also have, among other things, topiary, statuary, stone vases, box-edged paths and rows of cypresses. It is ironical that rows of Leyland cypress are now being planted in England because they make the quickest screen on the market. Unless clipped to resemble yew, these unhappy looking foreigners appear hopelessly out of place. Has anyone ever imagined what England will look like in fifty years when its villages and suburbs will be a forest of cypresses? I think plan-

ning permission should be needed before planting these trees and perhaps a tax paid to fund oaks.

Elizabethan gardeners laced their gardens with triangular, round and square beds but it was really Le Nôtre, gardener to Le Fouquet, one of Louis XIV's ministers, who was the grand master of bedding out. His gigantic formal parterre of elaborately shaped beds at Vaux-le-Vicomte was stuffed with brightly coloured flowers. His jealous employer copied the gardens on an even larger scale at Versailles and the royal army of gardeners sometimes worked all night to change the planting scheme from one set of colours to another so that, when the King opened his bedroom window in the morning (or had it opened for him), this pleasant surprise would render him instantly jolly. (The many new strains of annuals which keep appearing now would be enough to change the King's parterre every hour.)

The fashionable foibles of the large scale gardener, though a source of inspiration, are not necessarily followed by the small scale gardener who tends to stick to his guns through thick and thin and has a far clearer idea of what he likes. Gardening fashions among the horticultural élite wax and wane as dramatically as the moon. The eighteenth century, for instance, saw Kent and Brown sweep away formal gardens and replace them with fields, sheep, Wordsworthian lakes and

The design of the Leaders' garden in Hitchin, Hertfordshire has 'just grown over the years –
30 of them, in fact'. The bed full of annuals directly in front of the 1945 semi-detached
cottage has a completely different display each year.

rocky crags. By the 1800s the rich had grown bored with the 'picturesque' and the most dazzling beds of annuals once again burgeoned and abounded in the very latest gardens. The fast-growing suburbs could not be without mounded beds of lobelia, salvia and alyssum. Window boxes dripped with trailing geraniums and hanging baskets with begonias. As soon as this style became universal, the restless fashion seekers sought pastures new and began to decry gaudy swathes of colour and Gertrude Jekyll suggested hollyhocks and delphiniums. But there will always be a staunch bedding out brigade. It is a far more ancient form of gardening than the romantic muddle of lupins and old roses.

The small cottage garden, which only really evolved over the last two hundred years in a definable form, has sailed unabashed through these violent changes. Originally dependent to a considerable extent on gleaning tips and cuttings from the gardener at the big house up the road, the small gardener would not dispense plants or shrubs on a fashionable whim. Hence the wealth of topiary peacocks, fat hens and chess men who abound at cottage garden gates have kept their heads while all around were loosing theirs! The art of topiary, (begun by the Romans, who must have loved our indigenous box and yew when they were over here,) has taken on a new meaning in the last thirty years. Mr Rivers, a topiarist friend of mine whose garden has sadly gone, created a racehorse leaping the garden wall with a perfectly formed jockey up with his whip to hand and his cap pulled down. It was all made of privet and moved realistically when lorries passed along the nearby road. Mrs Stokes from Swanwick Green in Cheshire created an armchair out of a boring golden privet bush. She was so pleased that she went on to grow a living three piece suite on her lawn.

The design of a brilliant small garden may not always depend on kaleidoscopically arranged annuals or living architectural shapes but on the artful placing of artefacts and objects or by transporting the viewer into another world by literally creating . . . The shell garden at Southbourne is miraculous, as is the model village at Downton which is made of tiny cement houses stuck all over with broken china. The houses light up at night and at Christmas a recording of carols wafts from the miniature church across to the pavement where you stand amazed. My favourite garden is at Wimbourne where there is a small river running through the miniature village and a mill with a working wheel. No photograph can ever capture the wonder of those small worlds.

In larger worlds statues of mythological heroes and heroines have graced Hellenic glades from the very first beginnings of European pleasure gardens

Mr and Mrs J. Herbert's garden, Oxford Road, Long Itchington, near Rugby, with spectacular displays of polyanthus and tulips.

One of the topiary birds in Mr Heathman's garden at East Lambrook, Martock, Suffolk.

and were designed to transport you, if not to heaven, then on to a higher plane than earth. At each turn of the winding walk or at each vista's end you might expect to find a nymph or a shepherd. The trouble is that people like Diana the Huntress or Psyche may look fine in gardens or parkland where their scale suits grand buildings and woodland, but they do not belong in small gardens; neither do they have much to do with our folklore. Replicas of dogs, rabbits, ducks, tortoises, doves, boots and of course gnomes are the sorts of things you might expect to find in the garden anyway and, if they do not inspire sublimity, then they create a safe and homely atmosphere. A gnome brings good luck and has played an important part in our garden mythology for the last hundred years. In 1870 Sir Charles Isham of Lamport Hall in Northamptonshire brought one back from the Black Forest and made it the centrepiece of his magnificent rockery. That original gnome is still there to this day and from its mould hundreds and thousands of Lamport gnomes have been reproduced. Gnomes get mocked but their scale is right for a small garden. Whether you like them or not is up to you. If all England were covered in Grecian urns they would probably be deemed vulgar.

Colour and jollity lift the spirits. This is undeniable. So, of course, does beauty. If I am driving through Macclesfield in a drizzle, down a rather dull street and my thoughts are getting gloomy, which they tend to do, my mood can be instantly changed by the sight of a fantastic garden. It might be serene with full-blown rambling roses spilling over the porch like Mrs Frank's garden in Oxfordshire, or jolly like the Fishers' garden in Suffolk, packed with carefully painted animals and gnomes. I never look for one particular style of garden because that would make life so dull. *All the gardens in this book have made me the happier for seeing them.* Surely that is no mean feat!

The front garden giraffe in Mrs Williams' garden in Wellesbourne, Warwickshire is known as Victor and was her father's idea. When he was in his eighties, he was gazing through the window one day and he visualised the shape of this creature in the living ash tree.

Mr George Howard, the creator of this famous garden in Southbourne, Bournemouth, travelled all over the world and collected shells and momentoes from every corner.

# THE GARDENS

Mrs Rowley's garden in Bramber Road, Fulham, London

Mr Taysom has lived at Woodbine Cottage for 76 of his 77 years. A bachelor, he has been a keen amateur gardener since childhood and advises patience to gardeners, as success will then follow. Because of the riot of colour he displays through spring and summer he has scores of visitors. Staged on five tiers against the 18th-century cottage wall, he displays 120 large double begonias and 100 fuchsias. Bordering his path and lawns, he plants out approximately 3,500 annuals.

*Mr V Couch,*
*Bugle, St Austell, Cornwall*

LEFT Victor Couch has worked in the Cornish china-clay pits for most of his 89 years. He and his late wife came here when they were first married in their 20s, and they laid out the garden themselves. He cast the concrete dogs himself. 'I cast scores more of them and my wife used to say that the place was crawling with dogs.' Mr Couch's son now shares the house, which is in fact a London Underground railway carriage brought down by rail to Bugle over 60 years ago. 'Do a little gardening each day, it is a great hobby,' says Mr Couch.

*Mr and Mrs G. Purser,*
*Myrtle Grove, Box, Wiltshire*

This Marshall steam engine was converted in the War to sterilise top soil. Mr Purser liked the look of it and 'thought how nice it would look in our garden. At Christmas we have lights on the wheels which go on and off and make it look as though it is moving.'

*Mr S. Clark,*
*Box Lane, Minchinhampton, Stroud,*
*Gloucestershire*

❧❧❧

LEFT 'Because I'm a great royalist I always plan my front garden like this for any royal occasion. By June 1986 I knew that Fergie and Andrew's wedding was coming off and so I was able to plant out the garden just for them. It worked out just right for their wedding. I started by planting up the garden for the Queen's Jubilee, then I did beds for Princess Anne, Prince Charles and in 1982 I designed the garden just for the birth of Prince William. I always send photographs of my efforts to the royals and receive letters back which I treasure.'

*Mrs E. Clark,*
*Westonbirt, Tetbury, Gloucestershire*

❧❧❧

RIGHT Mrs Edith Clark, aged 89, has lived at the Old Post Office for 68 years. Her box hedges are over 110 years old. Mrs Clark says that the hard work she puts into the garden keeps her young and happy. Her son Stanley has inherited her love of gardening.

Mr Skelton, the gardener of the family, is 66 years old and creates one of the best bedding-out gardens in the Midlands each year. Not unnaturally he is a regular winner in the Sandwell Municipal Gardens competition, and in 1985 helped Sandwell to win the West Midlands Municipal Gardens Competition. Mr Skelton brings on 34 different varieties of bedding plants, and insists that he has no secrets other than using a hoe as much as possible when the bedding plants are still small. In fact he does have some secrets: he puts paper bags over his chrysanthemum heads to save them from rain damage and he grows his leeks very successfully in broken drainpipes.

## Mr and Mrs L. Hudson, Deddington, Oxfordshire

Leonard Hudson, an Austin-Rover factory worker, and his wife Sybil, have lived in 'Knotty Ash' for around 20 years. 'My wife was the inspiration in this garden as she so loves to be outdoors. We find that the pleasure it gives to us both by doing it in our spare time is well worth it. Many people call in for a friendly chat and a few tales of their own gardens. The smiles on the childrens' faces when they see the gnomes are worth everything.' The front garden at 'Knotty Ash' is filled with over 300 gnomes and animals which get placed differently after each weekly mowing of the lawn.

19

*Mr and Mrs D. Thompson,*
*Birchetts Green, Wadhurst, Sussex*

Daphne Thompson's 96-year-old mother who lives hard by, is still able to do a bit of weeding in this tumbling cottage garden spread-eagled before a tile-hung cottage so typical of Sussex. Daphne is definitely the head flower-gardener, and aims to keep things simple. 'The borders are in the true cottage-garden style, and I would advise people not to have more beds than they can cope with.'

## Mrs C. Franks,
### Steeple Aston, Oxfordshire

Mrs Franks has lived for 74 of her 77 years in this formerly thatched cottage. Her garden opens to the public in aid of the National Gardens Scheme and she is most adamant about retaining the look of a traditional cottage garden. 'Always use a push hoe on the garden to free all the weeds,' she says. 'Burn all the rubbish, don't leave it around. Prune shrubs and try to keep them in shape and try and get all the digging done before winter. Dress with lime wherever possible, but not where potatoes are going. Take as many cuttings and save as many kinds of seeds as you can for next year. My own seeds germinate in about 5 days, but the seed you can buy takes at least 10 to 14 days. Wash all flowerpots before storing away. Keep a continuation of colour in the beds right through the year – that's what makes a cottage garden.'

*Mr and Mrs W. Mayes,*
*Chapel Hill, Bollingey, Perranporth,*
*Cornwall*

On the road side of their 1933 asbestos-built
bungalow, Mr Mayes creates an incredible display
of godetias, verbenas, lobelias, french marigolds,
eschschotlzia and brachycomes, which is hardly
surprising as his expertise comes from long experi-
ence of working in the Parks department in the
warm, palmy town of Falmouth. He made all the
hanging baskets and window boxes himself, many
from four-litre ice-cream containers. 'My husband
laughed at me when I said I was going to nominate
our front garden,' says Birmingham born Mrs
Mayes, who writes for the *Daily Mirror* bimonthly
on rural topics, signing herself 'Old Codger', and
also writes nature books as Nellie Mayes. 'All the
holiday-makers certainly stop in their tracks at our
glow of colour outside this little four-roomed
shack.'

*Mrs G. Harding,*
*Peckforton, Tarporley, Cheshire*

In Mrs Harding's garden, down the road from Peckforton Castle, stands a life-sized elephant with a replica of the castle on its back. It is carved from local sandstone quarried from the hill behind this Victorian estate cottage. Mrs Harding and her husband came here some 60 years ago and found the garden in a great state of neglect. 'The elephant was covered in ivy and we only found the sandstone path with its moulded kerbs by chance, while digging. At the moment my bush roses are "Lilli Marlene", "Evelyn Fison", "Dicksons Flame", "Queen Elizabeth", "Elizabeth of Glamis", "Peace", "My Love", "Whisky Mac", "Violet Carson", "Mary Sumner", and "Piccadilly" – some have no name. I have grown them from cuttings given to me, like a lot of my plants; they remind me of people long gone.'

## Mr Heathman,
### East Lambrook, Martock, Suffolk

❧

LEFT Ron Heathman started these topiary birds and bobbles of juniper, privet and hawthorn about twenty years ago. He works in the local council highways department and hence keeps abreast of all the gardens in the area. His advice is to keep the topiary tidy by cutting it very often.

## Mr and Mrs R. Quinney,
### High Street, Castle Donington, Derbyshire

❧

RIGHT 'We moved in six years ago and for five years have won first prize in the parish council's best front-garden competition. They have now given me the trophy to keep and disqualified me from further entry.' The design of the garden was dictated by the steep slope. Apart from about 1,000 summer annuals, the regular inhabitants of the garden include primroses, polyanthus, sempervivums, hebes, thymes, cistuses, lavenders and campanulas.

Harry Rayson says that the natural slope of his garden determined the landscaping and planning. 'I have planted many varieties of conifer for colour range, and my bedding out plants usually number around 1,600.' Mr Rayson was formerly an electrical engineer but has just begun to grow plants commercially. 'When growing geraniums from seed,' he says, 'my advice is to start very early. I always sow on Boxing Day.'

30

## Mr R. Lee,
### Knatchbull Road, Camberwell, London

❧

LEFT Mr Ricky Lee, a carpenter and joiner, has lived here all his 28 years. 'The Dutch Garden in the front was designed by my grandfather. He was called Mr Adrianous Matinous Timmerans, and was of Dutch origin. He bought this property in 1926 and called it Hoek van Holland which means Corner of Holland.'

## Mr and Mrs J. Burks,
### Edelston Road, Crewe, Cheshire

❧

RIGHT Ada Burks used to sing on the stage. Her front garden, which is mostly housed in containers, invariably wins the Crewe Gardens Competition. 'Year in and year out we win it,' she says, 'and one year the local newspaper headline read "How Ada Attracts The Tourists" over a large picture of the garden.' She and her husband take two to three hours a day bringing the garden inside in the evening and putting it out again in the morning.

## Miss J. Hogg,
## Hartland Road, Hornchurch, Essex

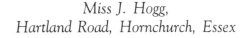

Joan Hogg believes that gardening is therapeutic and relaxing. Having become disabled with arthritis at the age of 45, Miss Hogg finds the garden keeps her going. 'It makes me face up to getting up when I might otherwise be tempted to stay down. My garden has made me friends, and many people say it brightens their day and cheers them up.'

## Mr and Mrs T. Hare,
## Cricket Ground Road, Norwich, Norfolk

Mr and Mrs Hare designed and built their bungalow, 'Baranto', 30 years ago. 'We designed the front garden,' says Tom Hare, the chief gardener, 'to be a little different from the usual – we have avoided straight paths and borders and included circular stepping-stones across the lawn to the front door. To avoid awkward corners, all areas close to the house have been cobbled to set off the tubs of flowers.' For his spring display he plants approximately 800 bulbs.

### Mrs and Mrs W. Abel,
### Netherhampton Road, Salisbury

❧❧❧

Mr and Mrs Abel came to their bungalow when it was built 30 years ago. Set beneath the chalk quarry between Salisbury and Netherhampton, the soil in the Abels' garden is not the easiest to deal with and in order to produce this prize-winning display (many times winners of Salisbury's Front Gardens Competition) they always add a lot of peat. The mainstays in the Abels' garden are roses, lavender, buddleia and cotoneaster.

### Mr and Mrs S. Wilks,
### Hartland Road, Hornchurch, Essex

❧❧❧

Mr Wilks spends all day in the garden outside his old age pensioner's bungalow. He plants 200 cwt. of tulips, snowdrops, daffodils, narcissus and crocuses, and in the summer he plants anything and everything. 'You name it, I've got it,' he says. 'I don't go in for all this uniform lark – if there's a hole I put a flower in it. I've also got 8 large chimney-pots, a fox and 4 cubs, 3 dogs, an old man, a birdbath, a seat, an old lady and a black cat. I like everything colourful and bright.'

*Mr and Mrs F. Barnfather,*
*Pembroke Avenue, Walkergate,*
*Newcastle upon Tyne*

'I just grew the ordinary green privet and kept this well shaped in the form of arches, but it grew so fast and became so wide and difficult, I decided to change to golden privet which is slower growing. I gave much thought to the shaping of this. I saw an advert in our local newspaper showing a silhouette of a ship, and from this I drew a plan to scale. When the hedge was about 2½ ft. high, I commenced the shaping; that would be about 19 years ago.' Mr Barnfather bought his house in 1934 as soon as the builders had completed it. 'I will never forget planting my first seeds and how thrilled I was when they eventually came up. When they reached maturity that first year they turned out to be weeds! You have to learn from your errors.'

Ernest Harris has lived all of his 70 years in this mid-18th century cottage. He usually spends up to five hours a week in his garden. 'I have a few daffodils and snowdrops, but I do like dahlias and French marigolds as they make a good colour for a long time. My tip for good gardening is to always use good farm muck, and never use any sprays from shops. Just use soft soap and water and this will kill all types of black and white fly.' Mr Harris stores his dahlia tubers upside down. 'They don't keep if they are the right way up. I always put them in the garden on the same day every year, Stow Fair day, which is generally 11 or 12 May. I keep the same ones every year and split them. I have some that my mother grew, and she's been dead forty years.'

*Mr and Mrs A. Tanner,*
*Kington St Michael, Wiltshire*

In the spring Mr Tanner's garden is ablaze with about half a hundredweight of mixed tulips and bulbs, while in the summer he plants out 800 bedding plants. 'I just like to keep a nice garden as there are six alms houses opposite with no front gardens and they can enjoy mine from their front windows. I like growing a few vegetables too. I also go for Kelso onions and I win the prize with them nearly every year. I show my sweet peas and chrysanthemums too. I've won the prize with them ten years in a row and I've won the Points Cup three years running.'

*Mrs S. Newington,*
*High Street, Rolvenden, Kent*

Sheila Marie Newington says her garden is a real hotchpotch. 'It's really a memory board of friends, or birthday presents. The winter jasmine was given to me when I moved in, and it was about 6 in. high. Now it flourishes and has reached my bedroom window. The rose on the house was here when I came 13 years ago and I cut it right down and tied it together like a faggot. Now it's all over the house and looks lovely. I have a wonderful gardening friend who comes and tidies me up when I have not been well, and I have helpful grandchildren aged from 25 down to 10. This garden has just grown like Topsy, and is full of bits and pieces given to me by friends.'

*Mr A. Dowdell,*
*Little Langford, Salisbury, Wiltshire*

Albert Dowdell created this perfect replica of
Stonehenge because he is a Wiltshire man and
wanted the county's most famous site near at
hand. It seemed easier to re-create than Salisbury
cathedral. He got the idea almost thirty years ago
when his bungalow was built on virgin land and he
was faced with creating a garden from scratch.

## Mr E. Prynn,
### Trevithick, St Merryn, Padstow, Cornwall

⋙❧

Eddie Prynn's front garden consists of a collection of gigantic stones named after certain women in his life. They include Aunty Hilda, Monica, Marjorie (his mother), Secret Lady, Jackie and Sally Brown, the music-maker. The stones are of granite, quarried from St Breward. There are also two blocks of quartzite blasted off Mount Pleasant in the Falklands, crated up and brought back to Cornwall by the contractors who built Stanley airport. 'I am turned on by rocks. If you run round the stone circle five times you feel as high as anything, as if you'd had a pint of beer.' Eddie Prynn describes his garden as a Druid Temple and performs his own form of 'ritual weddings'.

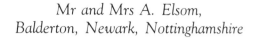

Arthur Elsom designed and built his own house in the evenings and at weekends. 'Never let up with your gardening, otherwise the weeds will win,' he says. 'However, sometimes when things are not going to plan, plants are failing or the work appears to be too much and a total stranger passing stops and says "Your garden always looks beautiful". Then I think gardening is worthwhile.'

*Mr and Mrs R. Dunn,*
*Crudwell, Malmesbury, Wiltshire*

Mr Dunn, a farm mechanic, looks after the garden with his wife and son, and says, 'It has just happened over the years.' The layout of the garden was dictated by the amount of concrete which had to be put in around the bungalow when the wooden foundations began to rot. 'Being an army hut originally designed for men manning the gunpost, which is still in the field by us, it was not built to last!' The Dunns plant 17 different varieties of dahlias which they keep from year to year; some have been swapped with friends and are referred to by the friends' names. 'The lady who lives opposite our gate gave us the pink one so we call it after her. We went to Stoke Festival this year and thought to ourselves, "My word, our dahlias are better than theirs."'

*Mr and Mrs S. Dix,*
*Hughes Close, Charlbury, Oxfordshire*

In 1986 the council threatened to cut off a large chunk of this garden to widen the road. Muriel and Sydney Dix, who have been married for 57 years and are both in their late 70s, were appalled by the state of the garden when they first came here 12 years ago. 'There were waist-high weeds and big heaps of rubbish under the windows. We looked at the mess with disgust and finally decided to get a load of good soil and plonk it on top after we had cleared off what we could. After much patience and perseverance our garden has reached its peak, so you can see we're a bit annoyed with the council, to say the least.'

## Mr W. Hampshire,
### Kirdford, Sussex

Mr Hampshire, an Evangelist, has created his garden around his cedarwood bungalow. It has now become a famous local sight and buses bound for Petworth pull up and stop so that their passengers can take in the 50 or so hanging baskets dripping with begonias. 'I'm 79,' says Mr Hampshire, 'and my wife is 80, and I have to say that her gloxinias are absolutely marvellous. She had 22 blooms on one the other day, and quite often has over 50 blooms on her streptocarpus. We get people from all over the world looking at our garden and one man from Japan addressed a letter to the man of the house of flowers, Kirdford, England, and it got here.'

Duncan Fisher has been in farming for most of his 80 years, and he and his friend Mrs Florence Stringer, assisted sometimes by Mr Henry Morley, work extremely hard in the garden. They keep the hoe going and the ground is regularly enriched with mushroom manure. 'We put nesting-boxes and bird-tables in strategic places around the garden, which makes gardening an even more pleasurable task.' A former Head Gardener of nearby Petworth House, the late Mr Fred Streeter, was responsible for the layout of the garden when he lived here in the 1950s. He also had a weekly gardening programme on the radio.

*Mr and Mrs A. Shirley,*
*Noke, near Oxford*

Violet Shirley's grandfather was born in this cottage in the 1800s, followed by her father and then herself. 'While being colourful,' she says, 'we also tend to be untidy, but we do like to think that ours is a country garden in keeping with our little country cottage. Our front garden was once a collection of farm implements and old sheds left behind by our grandparents, as it used to be a smallholding and wood business. My husband and I dismantled the old sheds and made the front garden.' Albert Shirley, a retired machinist, works an equal amount in the garden beside his wife Violet.

*Mr and Mrs D. Dyer,*
*Moor Lane, Cleveden, Somerset*

Dennis Dyer, a 57-year-old factory worker, does most of the gardening and manages to put in about two hours' work a day. His pantiled early 19th-century cottage needs this colourful display to set it off – 'I'm not afraid to pack bedding plants close together for a good carpet effect. I plant about 1,000 a year.'

## Mr and Mrs P. McDonagh, Hedgeman's Road, Dagenham, Essex

A neighbour said of Mr McDonagh, 'He's out here all the time. It's his life that boat, he lives for it.' Peter McDonagh insists that he is not a gardener. The topiary work is of privet and has taken about five years to cut into shape. 'It's a tug boat,' says Mr McDonagh, 'pulling a liner up river with a pilot boat in the rear, and also a large tramp steamer.'

## Mrs E. Jane, Golden Gear, Helford, Helston, Cornwall

Mrs Jane's cottage on the Helford River was once lived in by what she describes as 'a gang of trouble-some smugglers'. It was subsequently occupied by coastguards, then the Excise, until she and her husband came here in 1949. 'The garden is only waistcoat-pocket sized,' she says, 'and the topiary work is to commemorate a "tail down" Peacock engine which used to be at Gwinear Road Station before Doctor Beeching shut it down. I also have a wild-bird feeding enclosure because of kestrels.'

*Mr A. Powell,*
*Rangeworthy, Devon*

The late Mr Adrian Powell's topiary boat and train, which he grew over thirty years ago, will be trimmed regularly by the new owners of his house.

*Mr and Mrs A. Leach,*
*Main Road, Long Hanborough, Oxford*

Mr and Mrs Leach spend approximately 24 hours a week gardening in the summer. Mr Leach says what inspired him to create his garden was working in a nursery after leaving school. He then went into the Navy, which again inspired him to make what was once a straight hedge into the shape of HMS *Verity*, the ship on which he served. 'I felt it rather boring to keep cutting a straight hedge, so I just cut into it. I have also made a small stone lighthouse in the front, complete with light.'

Mrs R. Vallance,
*Kemp Road, Winton, Bournemouth, Dorset*

❧

LEFT  Over the years Ruby Vallance has tended to replace her bedding plants with plastic ones, and this year has only planted begonias in her front bed. The rest of the colour is made up with many antiques and bits and pieces she has picked up in local sales. 'I tend to keep children in mind as I like to attract their attention as they pass my house.'

Mr and Mrs J. Miles,
*The Borough, Downton, Salisbury, Wiltshire*

❧

RIGHT  Jack Miles' shell garden is a celebrated Wiltshire sight and many a coachload of tourists bound for Bournemouth diverts down the main street of Downton to view this miniature village. Mr and Mrs Miles often make trips to the seaside to collect shells, and get given enough broken china to go on building and maintaining the village. At Christmas each house and the central church is lit up and the lighting-up time has become a traditional event for the young children of Downton.

*Mr and Mrs F. Barker,*
*Brigsteer, Kendal, Cumbria*

The Barkers' National Trust cottage is part of the
Sizergh Castle Estate and stands close to the edge
of a lane which leads to nowhere in particular. The
cottage stands in border country which, until the
Union of 1603, was always in a state of flux. It was
known as the Debatable Land. In the summer
there is sometimes a queue of cars and buses
formed entirely of visitors stopping off at one of the
most breathtaking front gardens in the North of
England. The Barkers lived here for 35 years and
each did their fair share of gardening, as did their
daughters and grandchildren.

'People say the garden's something special, but to me it is ordinary,' said the late Mr Barker. 'We don't really notice it because we're here all the time. If we went away for a week and came back it would give us a surprise, but we never do go away. We garden in our sleep!' Having travelled the world in the navy, Mr Barker was happy to stay put in what a passer-by has described as being 'the nearest to heaven you will ever get'. When the vicar called by not long ago he said, 'My word, God's made a good job of your garden!' Mr Barker resisted saying 'You should have seen it when He had it to Himself.' Mrs Barker is keeping up the garden as her husband used to.

Mrs Stace's pride and joy is the duck house in the middle of her pond. It is not fixed to anything but floats among the water lilies. She used to let people into her garden to wander around, 'but would you believe,' says Mrs Stace, 'they kept pinching the gnomes.' The water lilies need an open and sunny position and are easily propagated by removing side shoots or by dividing the rhizomes.

*Mr and Mrs J. C. Downer,*
*New Road, Brixham, Devon*

'Through the summer months tourists in their charabancs are often diverted along this road into Brixham where they stop to view our garden and listen to their tour operator giving his commentary,' says Mrs Downer. 'The garden comes to life at the beginning of June every year when the flowers start to bloom and the figures are put out. The figures sit outside until the flowers die. Then they are fetched in ready to be cleaned and re-painted for next year.'

'The garden was completely derelict 23 years ago and seeing that it had a naturally steep slope we started at the bottom and worked our way up to the house. The design just semed to happen.' The Hales' garden, in the village of Fladbury overlooking the Avon, is open for people to walk round, and over £2,000 has been collected for cancer research in a box at the gate. 'The lily pool was full of fish until a heron ate them all in the winter of 1985. The lamp base originally stood by the old mill in Fladbury and the old pump came from a friend in the next-door village.'

*Mr S. Miller,*
*Robin Hood Way, Kingston, London*

Mr Miller is a retired master butcher. It has taken him 26 years to get his garden into this condition, which might make life dangerous for drivers on the A3 in and out of London. 'They pass this particular gem and don't keep their eyes on the road.' The villa was built in 1935, but Mr Miller added the teak and oak balcony to his bedroom after a visit to Switzerland had inspired him to do so 17 years ago. 'I grew the box pyramids from slips. It was a garden in New Malden which gave me the idea. I thought they would make a nice enclosure for my garden. The pyracantha which grows on the house looks good all the year round and is a lot better than having something that looks dead for half of it. I also think that it protects the house from the weather – it seems to keep it in very good condition. The stones on either side of the front gate are from the Cheddar Gorge.'

*Mr and Mrs E. Clark,*
*Wisborough Green, Billingshurst, Sussex*

Eric Clark has a small civil engineering business and he and his wife Jane work about 12 hours a week each at what they describe as their chosen hobby, gardening. 'Our garden is a part of our house and the environment in which we live. It is so restful after our business hassles, organising 25 men and having to spend so much time on crowded roads going from site to site.' The Clarks describe the design of their garden as purely following the natural contours. 'We look for weeds,' says Eric Clark, 'we don't let them look at us.'

*Mr J. Beveridge,*
*Branxton, Cornhill-on-Tweed,*
*Northumberland*

Mr Beveridge's concrete menagerie stands beside the site of the Battle of Flodden near the Scottish border. Around the strange figures are written quotations such as the following, beneath a cow:

'This has been a famous coo
Ten calves in twelve short years
Her carcass should make a savoury stew
Here is no cause for tears.'

The garden was inspired by the late Mr Fairnington, a master-joiner, who directed his employee James Beveridge to build this extraordinary fantasy.

## Mr J. Beveridge, Northumberland

The animals are based on drawings in children's books and are built up on an armature of 1 in. chicken netting stuffed with newspaper and with iron stays for legs. The rhinoceros, for instance, took two bags of cement mixed one to three with sand, and was built up in layers over several days. If Mr Fairnington saw an animal he fancied he would ask Mr Beveridge to make it in concrete. There is of course a shrine to Robert Burns.

*Mr D. Mumford,*
*Lower Brailes, Banbury, Oxfordshire*

❦

RIGHT Derek Mumford favours pink petunias
most years, which he has decided are the best
colour to blend with his golden ironstone cottage.
This warmth of colour in the stone is due to the
presence of oxide of iron and does indeed comple-
ment the petunias, which are natives of South
America.

*Mrs M. Holland,*
*Amberley, Arundel, Sussex*

❦

LEFT Marjorie Holland has lived in this chalk
and thatched cottage near the Sussex Downs for
58 years. 'I let things seed a lot,' she says, 'and
exchange plants with friends. I didn't design the
garden in the first place, it just happened. I love
colour in the garden and try to have it all the year
round. I grow some vegetables in the front to save
me going to the main vegetable garden as it is
down a steep slope and faces north. I come from
farming stock, my great-grandfather was a farmer
in Amberley.'

Mr and Mrs Lock, who are in their mid-40s, live in the ancient clothing and market town of Sudbury, where the painter Thomas Gainsborough's father had a cloth business. 'Don't try to copy anyone else,' says Mr Lock. 'Do your own thing and always try to have plenty of colour in your garden. It's my wife who makes all the colour here and she grows all the flowers from seed. I just do the grass cutting and edging. The garden attracts a lot of people during the summer months, which makes the time spent well worth while.'

*Mr and Mrs G. White,*
*Ashmere Rise, Sudbury, Suffolk*

When George White, a plumber, first came here seven years ago, his idea was to 'soften' the look of the bungalow. He added white splayed rendering under the windows, 'And then I put window boxes under the windows which further added to the "soft" look we were trying to achieve. We then felt that the paintwork did not blend in with the garden and changed the colour from green and white to a very delicate shade of primrose and white. I have been gardening for some 65 years. It's a hobby which I still enjoy. I'm not afraid to mix colours because nature's colours do not clash with each other.'

Mrs B. Martin,
*Wroslyn Road, Freeland, Oxford*

'My colourful floral display,' says Mrs Martin, 'is much admired by passers-by. I won the competition for the best-kept garden in Freeland in 1986. My favourite bedding plants are definitely busy lizzies; they have such a long flowering period, and of course I like the pink ones best – well, you can see I'm fond of pink! Here's what I planted for this summer: 300 begonia semperflorens, 80 impatiens, 40 cineraria maritima, 50 ageratum, 200 lobelia, 50 tuberous begonias, fuchsias, geraniums, 18 assorted roses, 1 viburnum, 1 laburnum, 1 ceanothus, 1 cotinus coggygria.

*Mr and Mrs D. Ahern,*
*Spears Cross Guest House, Dunster,*
*Somerset*

The Aherns inherited this garden when recently they bought the hotel. It was Mr Pluck who created it. 'Eighteen years ago there was no garden so I terraced it up and built a little cottage for one of my grandchildren. It looked so nice nestling in the flowers that I built another one and then I just went on adding.'

*Mr and Mrs W. Fisher,*
*Cookley, Halesworth, Suffolk*

Wilfred Fisher has been a farm-worker all his life and began this collection of ornaments about ten years ago when, playing Bingo, he won a model squirrel. His wife Dulcie says, 'All my pot plants died so we started collecting more ornaments as time went by. Wilfred makes a lot of them by using moulds he sends off for. The penguin, dog, fish, fox and mermaid are all his. They're made of concrete and then painted by him. We've got about a hundred ornaments now.'

*Mr E. Careless,*
*Oldbury Road, Rowley Regis, Warley,*
*Warwickshire*

❧

LEFT This Victorian whitewashed cottage has been the home of Mr Careless, a retired tube-fittings screwer, for 56 years, and he and his two sons look after the garden together. They plant over 200 bulbs each year for a spring display and have made a feature of their Cypress trees, moulding them into homely shapes. All the dahlias are meticulously labelled each year and the peas are famous in the area for regularly reaching a height of 8 ft.

*Mr and Mrs E. W. Harris,*
*Coleford, Crediton, Devon*

❧

RIGHT 'Visitors on holiday from as far away as America and Canada have taken photographs of our cottage and garden. Some have returned each year to see the different way of planting. My wife and myself plan it to blend with the old building. I've lived in the village all my life,' says Mr Harris, 'and come from a third generation of keen gardeners.'

71

LEFT 'Having a boggy corner as a front garden, we decided to make a large pool with a smaller one each end, thus producing two small waterfalls. We then put in a cider-mill which came from a nearby farmhouse, and we have made steps and beds to cope with the small slope of the site. My plants are like old friends to me.'

RIGHT Mr Murrish's family have lived in and around St Agnes for 600 years. From the Atlantic, high winds blow relentlessly across his garden, and in consequence much of Mr Murrish's garden is made up of decorative cooking-ranges and fireplaces, all restored in black with designs picked out in silver. 'It is an unusual garden,' he says, 'and serves well to stop speeding vehicles as well as creating a lot of interest to the younger generation. One fireplace in particular has polished brass which needs cleaning every week.'

Ruby Herbert has worked part-time in the local Co-op stores for some 30 years, and her husband John is a carpenter by trade. When they first designed and built their house over 35 years ago, the old locals told them that they would never grow anything in their garden for it had been used as a dump by the local sawmills and was about 6 ft. high with nettles and weeds. 'But we went to work and the second year we won the village award of "Best Kept Garden". This, of course, spurred us on.' The Herberts' spring display is as spectacular as their summer one, with its 5,000 polyanthus and 1,200 red Apeldoorn tulips. Though they have changed the sorts of flowers over the years this summer their garden sported 5,000 fibrous begonias, 500 silver leafs, 1,000 green moss and 35 standard fuchsias. 'Always keep one step in front of the garden,' says Ruby. 'Never let it get one step in front of you.'

The pair of topiary birds in Mr Tim Edey's garden are particularly delightful. Their heads and bodies have been tightly trimmed but the tails are left to grow freely.

Mr and Mrs A. Mills,
*Horringer, Bury St Edmunds, Suffolk*

❦

Two of the most famous yew birds in England flank the entrance of this pink-washed Suffolk cottage, which was the home of the Head Gardener of Ickworth House. Ornamental topiary like this went out of fashion in large gardens during the 18th century. The tradition of its presence in cottage gardens, however, has remained unshaken. It is doubtful that the creator of these birds intended them to be quite as large as they now are.

### Mrs O. Bannister,
### Clopton, Wickhambrook, Newmarket, Suffolk

꙳꙳꙳

The late Mr Jack Bannister trained the may tree into a bird. He also built a model of Wickhambrook Village Church which stands underneath. The box hedge has been trained into a chicken by his daughter-in-law, Mrs Violet Bannister.'

### Mr E. Smith,
### Kidlington, Woodstock, Oxfordshire

꙳꙳꙳

Bill Smith's topiary work exemplifies English brilliance in this art. The best media for topiary are yew, box or privet because of their tight growing habit. You can either cut into existing bushes or plant from scratch. If you are in a hurry it is best to plant the three or five shrubs of your choice close together. Sit and watch for a year or two and then, unless you are brave with your razor-sharp shears and artistic to boot, find your nearest good piece of topiary work and ask its owner what to do next.

*Mrs S. Howard,*
*Southbourne Overcliffe Drive, Southbourne,*
*Bournemouth, Dorset*

The creator of this famous shell garden, Mr George Howard, died recently, but it is still visited daily by hundreds of people in the summer months. Mr Howard worked in a coal-mine in South Wales from the age of 15, and some of his equipment is displayed in the garden. He then travelled all over the world and collected shells and mementoes from every corner. He landed up in Bournemouth in the early 1930s with seven shillings and sixpence in his pocket, and eventually began the shell garden which he never stopped adding to. It is full of caverns, fountains, seats, shrines, statues, mottoes and quotes.

### Mr and Mrs W. Gill,
### Greenhill Avenue, Lympstone, Devon

William Gill has been the chief gardener for some
20 years. Petunias are his mainstay, while he varies
the other annuals such as marigolds, begonias and
fuchsias each year. He tends to plant from 1,500
to 2,000 annuals a year. 'I use cannas and ricinus
as 'dot' plants to give what I think is a slightly
tropical effect and to break up the annuals. I also
have two wheelbarrows which I display with vari-
ous plants in them. I like to get as much colour as I
can packed into the beds and believe that one of
the most important things in my garden is the lawn
– only the grass being the colour it is can show off
the flowers to the best. Our garden is there to be
enjoyed by passers-by.'

## Mrs E. Cassell,
### Amyruth Road, Brockley, London

Her Royal Highness, the Queen Mother, visited Elinor Cassell's garden when she won the All London Cup in the London Gardens Society's competition. 'My garden is a joy to me, both for the pleasure I get in growing all my plants from seeds or cuttings, and for the pleasure it gives to the many people who come each year to see it.' Mrs Cassell has been described as 'a lady who brought more honour and glory to the London Gardens Society than it has ever known.' Her tip is quite simply: 'Use one's own intuition – don't always go by the book.'

## Mr and Mrs H. Waterhouse,
### High Street, Ticehurst, East Sussex

⤛⤜

LEFT Mr and Mrs Waterhouse keep their garden up to a very high standard because 'we just love it'. The azaleas were planted over 30 years ago. 'They know we're getting old and can't look after them as we used to. Still, they say to us, "you just keep quiet and we'll be all right".' Harold Waterhouse has lived in this typical Kentish tile-hung cottage for all his 80 years.

## Mr M. Black,
### Chalfont Road, Oxford

⤛⤜

RIGHT Michael Black, a sculptor, works in the garden in front of his 1890 house for approximately ten days in each year. His plants include giant hogweed, giant silver thistles, briony, gold vine, deadly nightshade and a Kiftsgate rose. 'I scrounge a lot of plants and cuttings off friends and am most interested in varieties of green. I have a hayfield full of flowers for a lawn until September when it is cut twice into a proper lawn for the autumn. I think you should come to terms with your "weeds".'

John Sheard, an 86-year-old retired coal-miner, makes everything from throwaway materials like plastic containers, motor tyres and stuff which comes off the builder's skip. 'It has got to be something for nothing; I am already called Steptoe. My gardening started in 1914 and when the war broke out they turned the field at the back of the school into allotments and we learned the art of bastard trenching.' Mr Sheard makes all his own plant pots out of plastic bags, fusing the plastic with a hot skewer and thus making drainage holes at the same time.

*Mr W. Crossbates,*
*Breedon-on-the-Hill, Leicestershire*

Mr Crossbates did not have any particular plan in mind when he started his garden over 30 years ago. It has just gradually evolved, and he derives great pleasure from the amount of children who come to gaze at his creation. The weathervane in the foreground is on a 10-ft. pole and moves with the wind. Breedon has been inhabited since Iron-Age settlers made a hill-fort of it, but nowadays over half the hill, which is made of limestone, has been quarried away to form road metalling.

*Mr H. Barnfield,*
*The Green, Frampton-on-Severn,*
*Gloucestershire*

'I'm no gardener, I mean I was at sea all my life and I don't know the first thing about gardening really. It just sort of happens, doesn't it?' Harold Barnfield has lived at the Red House for over 20 years and tries to vary his bedding scheme a little bit every year, though he always includes busy lizzies and begonias because they seem to suit the soil and don't dislike a bit of shade. He designed and built the dovecote when he first came here, and bought the cat which sits on top from a local nursery. 'I always had pigeons as a boy, and so I thought I'd try my luck with doves. Fantails roam all over the place and one day mine never came back. I now have about six pairs of Turbots.'

*Mr and Mrs B. Clifford,*
*Dymock, Newent, Gloucestershire*

'I love gardening because I enjoy the outdoor life,' says Mrs Clifford. 'It is also very relaxing and rewarding, especially as I live in the centre of a very pretty village which last year won the Bledisloe Cup for the best-kept medium-sized village in Gloucestershire. This year we won the competition for the best-kept garden in the village. There is a lot of hard work involved, especially as my husband has an artificial leg. We work little and often in the garden rather than doing long stints, and we divide the work up equally.'

## Mrs D. Steele,
## Wimborne Road, Wimborne, Dorset

Mr Steele, who died in 1984, began to create this garden in 1947 when he and his wife moved here. Both of them Dorset born and bred, they had met at 15 and married at 18. Their son and five daughters all live locally, and together with Mrs Steele, who is now 83, combine to maintain this extraordinary work of art. A replica of Braemar Castle is the focal point; it is made of concrete and its moat is filled with water which flows from a tap in the corner of the garden through a miniature millwheel with a working mill, and onwards round the garden. The chestnut tree, which is kept in a dwarf form, was grown from a conker brought home by young Master Steele nearly 40 years ago on his way back from his school on Middle Hill. The garden shed, just visible from the road, is smothered in hub-caps.

*Mr J. Coombes,*
*Dean Lane, Sixpenny Handley, near*
*Salisbury, Dorset*

❧

'I am interested in all aspects of nature, from insects to electrical storms. Some parts of the garden are adapted to support this. For instance, wild flowers such as ragged robin, pink campion, wild foxgloves and ladies' bedstraw are grown to attract the butterflies. The garden is designed to give colour 12 months of the year. When we came here, it was all straight borders, but my wife said it was much too regimental, so I have made everything with curved edges. To stop the slugs attacking my delphiniums I cover the crowns in early spring with a layer of peat – they won't cross it to eat the shoots and it seems to work on most plants.'

*Miss E. Rice,*
*Hoskins Road, Oxted, Surrey*

'I can't be bothered with names of plants,' says Elizabeth Rice. 'I grow what I like and move plants any old time, but I always water them in well. My dog and garden are my loves in life and my dog is not allowed in the front garden but has the run of the back.' A neighbour, Mrs Agnes Guthrie, recommended Miss Rice's garden as being 'a delight to all who pass by'. Miss Rice has lived in 'Owlets' for over 20 years, as did her sister until she died four years ago. It was Miss Elizabeth who was the gardener, though. 'My sister never helped in the garden but always kept the paths swept. I work about three hours a day in the summer months, and my advice is love your garden and deadhead all the time.'

## Mr and Mrs D. Miller,
### Rowney Gardens, Dagenham, Essex

Mr and Mrs Miller have probably won more front-garden competitions than anyone else in the country. Their prizes have included a visit from Eric Morecambe and Ernie Wise, who had tea on their lawn; a visit to San Francisco, and another to Honolulu. Mr and Mrs Miller do not divulge all their secrets, 'but one good tip,' says Daphne, 'is to vary the plants' diet. If you are getting the same food all the time, you get cheesed off, and when you've got so many plants packed together they are taking a lot out of the soil.' Every three or four years the Millers' garden is left to lie fallow in the spring and they plant no bulbs or wallflowers that year. The inspiration to create a garden of this rare quality came from the need to 'brighten a dreary environment,' says Mrs Miller.

## Mr F. Long,
### Mason's Road, Stratford-on-Avon, Warwickshire

Frederick Long made his garden from nothing over a period of seven months after moving to this warden-controlled council bungalow. Apart from window boxes, hanging baskets and urns, he also has a plastic donkey with two flowerpots on its back, a windmill and a concrete duck. 'I keep at it every day.'

## Mr and Mrs H. Sweet,
### Locks Hill, Frome, Somerset

Mr Sweet, a retired builder, built his own bungalow with terracing in front especially designed for bedding out. His wife, who worked in the bookbinding department of a local printer for 40 years, does the digging while Mr Sweet beds out the 800 plants each year. A hundred geraniums go out and Mr Sweet keeps 200 back in the greenhouse in case the ones in the front need replacing. In 1981 the Sweets received a plaque from America for 'Helping to Beautify the World'.

95

*Mr and Mrs W. Hall,*
*Charlton, Singleton, Chichester, Sussex*

Mr Hall looks after the vegetables. His onions win prizes at all the local shows. Mrs Jensen, an admiring neighbour, doubts that larger ones are grown anywhere else in the country. Mrs Hall looks after the flowers and adds each year to the spring display of daffodils, crocuses, tulips, anemones, scillas and snowdrops, while in the summer she relies heavily on annuals. The latter supplement her already established cistus, day lilies, campanulas, sidalcea, trollius, delphiniums, marguerites, montbretia, phlox, perennial foxglove, Jacob's ladder, columbines, pansies, dianthus and many others. 'It is only a simple cottage garden, but I like to think it's good because we give it such a lot of TLC (tender loving care!). I walk round it several times a day and do whatever is necessary,' says Mrs Hall.

96

*Mr and Mrs R. Wilkins and Mrs F. Compton,*
*Hampton Street, Tetbury, Gloucestershire*

❧⟫⟫⟫⟫

LEFT This joint effort of bedding out plants up the communal path has been going on for over 30 years. The tile-hung pair of cottages were built in 1921 from materials from the nearby aerodrome of Leighterton. In the spring the borders are ablaze with narcissi, wallflowers and primoses.

*Mr and Mrs A. Edwards,*
*Fulbrook, Burford, Oxfordshire*

❧⟫⟫⟫⟫

RIGHT Mr Edwards is a retired electrical engineer and says that the results in his garden are achieved through the joint efforts of his wife and himself. Syston, their house, was also designed by both of them, and was built in 1956. The Edwards' speci-alities are dahlias and asters. The dahlia belongs to the same family and the same country as the potato, namely Mexico. The Edwards' secret for healthy dahlias is to put a lot of peat in the soil and to give an annual dressing of mushroom compost.

Reuben Smith is a retired horticulturalist and prefers to spend no time at all working in the garden – 'None, if I can help it.' He leaves it up to his wife. His great-grandfather, Simon Smith was a traveller in beaver hats and bought this house in 1853. A photograph taken of the house in the 1890s shows the yew trees at almost the same height as now. They are clipped once a year in September with electric hedge trimmers and the whole operation takes three days.

100

# Acknowledgements

Lots of thanks to Mrs Barker and the late Mr Barker, Blounts Garden Centre, Andrew Parker Bowles, Dennis Bruce, William and Sarah Bulwer-Long, Mrs Burnett, Stan Chivers, Rodney Cook, Colin Farmer, John Glover, Mr Hancock, Ruby and John Herbert, Tony Isham, Gladys Jackson, Miss Johnston, Nancy Lancaster, Robin Lane Fox, Briony, Karina and Susanna Lawson, Lucy, Imogen, Endellion, David, John and Rupert Lycett Green, Enid McIlveen, Sheila McKnight, Carol Mace, Mr Menhinick, David Milnaric, Mrs Monnegan, Mr Moulton, Mr Newman, Terry Nightingale, Rachel Robbins, Ray Smith, Mrs Steele, Sandra Urban, David Vicary, Ray Witherspoon.

We would particularly like to thank Beautiful Britain in Bloom, an organisation sponsored by Barratt Developments, and their London co-ordinator Jenny Crosland, together with Mrs J. Atkinson.

# BIBLIOGRAPHY

If you feel inspired to venture further with your garden, the best thing you can do is to look at as many other gardens as possible and to ask questions, particularly on matters of topiary and model making. There are no books in existence which are as helpful as a neighbouring expert might be on these subjects.

The best books on bedding plants are the seed catalogues. Their vivid pictures and descriptions and planting information are really all you need to know. For the layout of flower beds you might be inspired by the National Trust book *Recreating the Period Garden*, published by Collins, which is a very good and practical guide. *Cottage Garden Flowers* by Margery Fish (Faber & Faber) takes a lot of beating if you are after the informal look. *Pergolas, Arbors, Gazebos, Follies* by David Stephens (Ward Lock) has some zany ideas.

If you want to be a good gardener and smile a lot, never stop reading Robin Lane Fox and Rosemary Verey.

# Index

# Index